Considering ADHD As Opportunity

Turning Obstacles into Success

Joshy Degb

Contents

Copyright © 2024 by JOSHY DEGB

All rights reserved. No part of this publication may be reproduced, distributed, or transmitted in any form or by any means, including photocopying, recording, or other electronic or mechanical methods, without the prior written permission of the publisher, except in the case of brief quotations embodied in critical reviews and certain other non-commercial uses permitted by copyright law.

Introduction: Unleashing Your Potential

ADHD Reframed as an Opportunity

Imagine a world where characteristics are commonly perceived as hindrances which transform into the very driving forces behind remarkable achievements. This is a potential reality that individuals with attention deficit hyperactivity disorder (ADHD) may face. ADHD, often misunderstood and stigmatized, is not simply a collection of symptoms. It represents a distinct cognitive processing style that holds great untapped potential. By shifting the perspective on ADHD from a perceived limitation to a unique advantage, a pathway to exceptional achievement and personal growth can be revealed.

An essential aspect of this reframing is rooted in

comprehending the scientific principles behind ADHD. Extensive research has shown that individuals with ADHD frequently display unique neurological characteristics that can result in notable strengths. For example, variations in brain structure and function can contribute to increased creativity, flexible problem-solving skills, and an exceptional ability to concentrate on tasks that pique their interest. Let's examine the case of David Neeleman, the founder of JetBlue Airways. He credits his ADHD for providing him with unique perspectives that have contributed to his innovative thinking and business success. Understanding the scientific foundations allows individuals to perceive their ADHD not as a disorder but as a reservoir of distinctive capabilities.

An empowering aspect of ADHD is its potential to transform challenges into opportunities for achievement. Individuals with ADHD often exhibit impulsivity and high energy, which can lead them to take risks and seize opportunities that others may be more hesitant to pursue. As an illustration, Michael Phelps, the renowned Olympic swimmer, directed his high energy towards intensive training and competitive events, resulting in his remarkable achievements that shattered records. When effectively addressed, these challenges can serve as valuable sources of motivation and tools for attaining exceptional results.

Managing daily life with ADHD can be challenging, but by implementing effective strategies, these challenges can be transformed into opportunities. Implementing structured routines, practicing mindfulness, and utilizing technology for organization are several effective strategies that can enhance focus and productivity. Tim Ferriss, an accomplished author and entrepreneur, utilizes precise time-management techniques that are tailored to his ADHD condition. As a result, he is able to effectively handle multiple high-stakes projects. These techniques illustrate that by employing the appropriate methodology, one can leverage the attributes of ADHD to improve daily productivity.

Building a strong support network is essential for individuals with ADHD, as success is rarely achieved in isolation. Seeking support from individuals in your personal network as well as experts in the field can provide valuable encouragement and guidance to help you navigate challenges and make the most of opportunities. This network offers a wide range of perspectives, ensures accountability, and fosters a strong sense of community. For example, actor Ryan Gosling attributes his successful career and ability to manage his ADHD to the support of his family. Constructing such a network is crucial in converting ADHD from an individual challenge into a collective path of development and achievement.

Individuals with ADHD may encounter unique challenges in professional and academic environments. However, these settings also offer significant opportunities for success.

Creating environments that acknowledge and support the strengths of individuals with ADHD can lead to their success, both in the workplace and in educational settings. Google and Apple are well-known for their inclusive policies that foster creative and unconventional thinkers. Personalized learning approaches and adaptive technologies have the potential to greatly benefit students. Jessica McCabe, an accomplished author and highly regarded motivational speaker, has utilized her expertise in ADHD to develop "How to ADHD," a comprehensive platform that provides valuable resources to individuals seeking to better comprehend and harness the power of their ADHD.

Having a strong sense of self-awareness can be instrumental in harnessing the potential of ADHD and turning it into a remarkable asset. Reflective and interactive exercises, such as journaling, meditation, and goal-setting, can assist individuals in gaining insight into their distinct patterns and triggers. Having a clear understanding of oneself is crucial for taking strategic action and fostering personal growth. The journey is both personal and inspiring, as demonstrated by numerous success stories.

In essence, the concept of reframing ADHD as an opportunity involves acknowledging and utilizing inherent strengths instead of disregarding the associated challenges. Through a deep understanding of the science behind ADHD, a willingness to embrace challenges, the implementation of practical techniques, the establishment of a strong support network, and the ability to achieve success in structured environments, individuals with ADHD have the potential to turn perceived obstacles into remarkable achievements. It is possible to embark on a path towards harnessing ADHD as a unique strength that serves as a source of motivation and encouragement. This journey showcases that by adopting the appropriate mindset and utilizing effective strategies, what was previously perceived as a disorder can be transformed into a valuable asset in the pursuit of achievement.

The Way Forward

Individuals diagnosed with Attention Deficit Hyperactivity Disorder (ADHD) possess unique qualities that can be harnessed as advantages, leading to exceptional accomplishments. This perspective holds true in a world where challenges are redefined and overcome. ADHD is a complex neurological condition that is often misunderstood and stigmatized. It is important to recognize that it is not simply a set of symptoms, but rather a unique condition with great potential. By adopting an alternative perspective, it is possible to alter our perception of ADHD and leverage it as a driving force for achievement. Instead of perceiving it as a constraint, we can regard it as a chance to surmount challenges and accomplish our objectives.

An essential aspect of this transformative viewpoint involves gaining a comprehensive understanding of the scientific principles underlying ADHD. Neuroimaging studies have provided insights into the unique brain structures and functions observed in individuals with ADHD. Notably, these studies have highlighted differences in regions like the prefrontal cortex, which plays a crucial role in executive functions such as decision-making, impulse control, and attention regulation. These neurological differences, which are frequently viewed in a negative light, actually contribute to the development of distinct strengths. For example, ADHD has been found to potentially enhance creativity and problem-solving abilities. David Neeleman, the founder of JetBlue Airways, attributes his innovative thinking and business acumen to his ADHD, which he sees as a valuable asset rather than a limitation.

Recent genetic research has provided valuable insights into the biological underpinnings of ADHD, revealing a significant hereditary component. Various studies have identified a number of genes associated with the regulation of neurotransmitters, including dopamine and norepinephrine. These genes play a critical role in attention and behavior control. These genetic findings have the potential to improve the accuracy of ADHD diagnosis and enable personalized treatment strategies that are tailored to an individual's genetic makeup. This can lead to more effective and targeted interventions.

Environmental factors are important contributors to the development and expression of ADHD. There is a clear and objective link between prenatal exposure to toxins such as tobacco smoke and alcohol, low birth weight, and early childhood adversity and an increased risk of developing ADHD. Understanding these risk factors highlights the significance of public health interventions that target these influences during crucial developmental stages. This, in turn, can help decrease the occurrence and intensity of ADHD.

The role of diet and nutrition in managing ADHD symptoms is gaining recognition as a significant factor. Studies indicate that a lack of essential nutrients such as omega-3 fatty acids, iron, and zinc can potentially worsen the symptoms associated with ADHD. On the other hand, dietary interventions that incorporate these nutrients have demonstrated potential for reducing symptoms and enhancing overall functioning. Incorporating nutritional strategies into comprehensive treatment plans can improve the overall well-being of individuals with ADHD, emphasizing the significance of a holistic approach to management.

Pharmacological treatments are still considered essential in managing ADHD, and ongoing advancements are continuously improving these approaches. Stimulant medications like methylphenidate and amphetamines are well-known for their effectiveness in enhancing attention and decreasing hyperactivity and impulsivity. Non-stimulant medications such as atomoxetine and guanfacine are increasingly recognized for their effectiveness, especially for individuals who do not respond well to stimulants or experience adverse side effects. Continued research on the pharmacodynamics and long-term effects of these medications is crucial for enhancing treatment regimens and reducing potential risks.

In addition to pharmacological interventions, behavioral therapies have demonstrated significant potential for effectively managing symptoms associated with ADHD. Cognitive-behavioral therapy (CBT) has been widely researched and proven to be an effective approach. It assists individuals in developing coping strategies, improving executive functioning, and reducing comorbid conditions like anxiety and depression. Advancements in technology have enabled the creation of digital cognitive-behavioral therapy (CBT) programs and mobile applications, enhancing the accessibility and engagement of these therapeutic interventions. These digital interventions offer interactive platforms for individuals to practice and reinforce skills learned in therapy, providing a modern and effective complement to traditional treatment methods.

Recent advancements in the field of neurofeedback and brain stimulation techniques have opened up promising avenues for the management of ADHD. Neurofeedback is a technique that focuses on training individuals to modify their brain wave patterns by providing them with real-time feedback. The ultimate goal of this training is to improve attention and self-regulation abilities. Research findings indicate positive outcomes, as individuals exhibited long-lasting enhancements in ADHD symptoms after undergoing neurofeedback training. In recent studies, researchers have been investigating the potential benefits of non-invasive brain stimulation techniques like transcranial magnetic stimulation (TMS) and transcranial direct current stimulation (tDCS) in enhancing neural plasticity and cognitive function. The use of these advanced methods presents promising opportunities for non-pharmacological interventions that focus on the fundamental neural mechanisms of ADHD.

Recent research has also placed significant emphasis on studying the educational and occupational outcomes of individuals with ADHD. Customized educational interventions, such as individualized education plans (IEPs) and classroom accommodations, have been found to have a substantial positive impact on academic performance and behavior management in students with ADHD. Workplace accommodations, such as flexible scheduling, task modifications, and assistive technology, have been shown to improve job performance and increase job satisfaction for adults with ADHD. The findings highlight the significance of establishing supportive environments that acknowledge and accommodate the distinct requirements of individuals with ADHD, thus promoting their potential for achievement in academic and professional contexts.

It is essential to have a comprehensive understanding of the coexistence of ADHD with other psychiatric and developmental disorders in order to provide effective treatment. ADHD often occurs alongside conditions like anxiety, depression, learning disabilities, and autism spectrum disorder. Understanding the relationship between ADHD and these comorbidities is crucial for creating treatment plans that effectively address all aspects of an individual's requirements. Recognizing and addressing comorbid conditions at an early stage can greatly enhance long-term results, underscoring the significance of a comprehensive and integrated treatment approach.

Recent research has led to significant changes in public awareness and societal attitudes toward ADHD. Enhanced comprehension of the neurological and genetic foundation of the condition has contributed to the reduction of stigma and the promotion of acceptance of ADHD as a valid and controllable condition. Organizations like CHADD (Children and Adults with Attention-Deficit/Hyperactivity Disorder) and ADHD Europe have made significant contributions to raising awareness, providing support to individuals and families, and influencing policy changes to enhance access to diagnosis and treatment.

There is a growing recognition of the benefits of mindfulness and physical exercise for individuals with ADHD. Research has demonstrated that engaging in mindfulness practices, such as meditation and yoga, can enhance attention, emotional regulation, and overall well-being. In addition, consistent physical exercise has been linked to a decrease in symptoms of ADHD and an improvement in cognitive abilities. The incorporation of holistic approaches into traditional treatment plans provides a comprehensive strategy for effectively managing ADHD.

Individuals with ADHD can benefit from a shift in their perception and management of the condition. Through a comprehensive understanding of the science behind ADHD, a willingness to embrace its challenges, the implementation of practical management techniques, the establishment of strong support networks, and the ability to thrive in structured environments, individuals with ADHD have the potential to turn perceived obstacles into remarkable achievements.

This journey towards harnessing the power of ADHD showcases the remarkable potential that lies within every individual. It serves as a testament to the fact that, with the appropriate mindset and resources, what was once perceived as a disorder can be transformed into a unique advantage in the pursuit of achievement. As research progresses, it holds the potential for significant advancements that can greatly improve the quality of life for individuals with ADHD and their families.

CHAPTER 1

THE SCIENCE OF ADHD

Recent Research and Findings

Advancements in research have greatly enhanced our comprehension of Attention Deficit Hyperactivity Disorder (ADHD), a condition that is often complex and misunderstood. Recent developments have led to a shift in perspective regarding ADHD. It is no longer seen solely as a disorder but rather as a distinct neurological profile that presents both challenges and strengths. By thoroughly examining current scientific research, we can gain a deeper understanding of ADHD and its complex nature. This knowledge can then be used to develop effective strategies for harnessing the inherent strengths associated with ADHD.

An important development in ADHD research is the

discovery of its neurological foundations. Research utilizing neuroimaging techniques, such as functional MRI (fMRI) and positron emission tomography (PET) scans, has uncovered notable disparities in the brain structures and functions of individuals diagnosed with ADHD. There are notable differences in the size and activity levels of specific brain regions, particularly the prefrontal cortex. This area plays a crucial role in executive functions like decision-making, impulse control, and attention regulation. Having a clear understanding of these neurological differences is crucial in order to develop precise interventions that can improve cognitive and behavioral outcomes for individuals with ADHD.

Genetic research has been instrumental in revealing the biological underpinnings of ADHD. Research conducted through twin and family studies has consistently demonstrated that ADHD has a strong hereditary component. Genetic factors play a substantial role in determining the likelihood of developing this condition. A number of genes have been identified by researchers that are linked to the regulation of neurotransmitters, including dopamine and norepinephrine. These neurotransmitters play a critical role in the regulation of attention and behavior. Genetic insights have proven to be valuable in enhancing the accuracy of ADHD diagnosis and opening up possibilities for personalized treatment strategies tailored to an individual's genetic profile.

Another significant area of recent research focuses on the impact of environmental factors on the development and expression of ADHD. There is a well-established correlation between prenatal exposure to toxins, such as tobacco smoke and alcohol, low birth weight, and early childhood adversity, and an elevated likelihood of developing ADHD. It is crucial to address environmental risk factors through public health interventions and policies that aim to reduce exposure to potential hazards during critical periods of development.

These findings highlight the significance of taking action in this regard.

Recent studies have emphasized the significance of diet and nutrition in relation to ADHD symptoms, alongside genetic and environmental factors. Studies have shown that a lack of specific nutrients, including omega-3 fatty acids, iron, and zinc, can worsen the symptoms of ADHD. On the other hand, dietary interventions that incorporate these nutrients have demonstrated potential for decreasing symptoms and enhancing overall functioning. This research provides strong evidence for incorporating nutritional strategies into comprehensive treatment plans for individuals with ADHD.

Pharmacological treatments for ADHD have been widely used to manage symptoms for a significant period of time. Ongoing research has led to advancements in these approaches, further enhancing their effectiveness. Stimulant medications, such as methylphenidate and amphetamines, continue to be widely prescribed treatments. Research consistently demonstrates their effectiveness in enhancing attention and decreasing hyperactivity and impulsivity. In addition to stimulant medications, non-stimulant alternatives like atomoxetine and guanfacine have been acknowledged for their efficacy. These medications are particularly beneficial for individuals who do not respond favorably to stimulants or encounter undesirable side effects. Continued research on the pharmacodynamics and long-term effects of these medications is essential for enhancing treatment regimens and reducing potential risks.

In addition to pharmacological interventions, behavioral therapies have demonstrated considerable potential for effectively managing symptoms associated with ADHD. Cognitive-behavioral therapy (CBT) has been thoroughly researched and proven to be an effective method for assisting individuals in developing coping strategies, enhancing executive functioning, and alleviating comorbid conditions like anxiety and depression. Advancements in technology have led to the development of digital cognitive-behavioral therapy (CBT) programs and mobile apps, which have increased the accessibility of these therapies to a broader population. These digital interventions provide individuals with interactive and engaging platforms to practice and reinforce the skills they have learned in therapy.

One area of research that shows promise is the use of neurofeedback and brain stimulation techniques to regulate brain activity in individuals with ADHD. Neurofeedback is a technique that focuses on training individuals to modify their brain wave patterns by providing them with real-time feedback. The ultimate objective is to improve attention and self-regulation abilities. Research findings indicate positive outcomes, as individuals consistently exhibited enhanced ADHD symptomatology subsequent to engaging in neurofeedback training. In recent studies, researchers have been investigating non-invasive brain stimulation techniques like transcranial magnetic stimulation (TMS) and transcranial direct current stimulation (tDCS) to determine their effectiveness in enhancing neural plasticity and improving cognitive function in individuals diagnosed with ADHD. These innovative methods present intriguing potential for non-pharmacological interventions that focus on the fundamental neural mechanisms of ADHD.

Recent research has also placed emphasis on examining the educational and occupational outcomes for individuals with ADHD. Research has demonstrated that customized educational interventions, such as individualized education plans (IEPs) and classroom accommodations, have been found to have a substantial positive impact on academic performance and can effectively reduce disruptive behaviors in students diagnosed with ADHD. In addition, workplace accommodations such as flexible scheduling, task modifications, and the utilization of assistive technology have been shown to improve job performance and job satisfaction among adults with ADHD. The findings emphasize the significance of establishing supportive environments that acknowledge and adapt to the distinct requirements of individuals with ADHD. This, in turn, promotes their potential for achievement in academic and professional contexts.

Investigating the comorbidity of ADHD with other psychiatric and developmental disorders is a crucial area of research. ADHD often accompanies other conditions, including anxiety, depression, learning disabilities, and autism spectrum disorder. It is crucial to have a clear understanding of the relationship between ADHD and these comorbidities in order to create thorough treatment plans that effectively address all aspects of an individual's requirements. A growing body of research has highlighted the significance of promptly identifying and intervening in comorbid conditions. This proactive approach has shown promising results in enhancing long-term outcomes for individuals with

ADHD.

Recent research has contributed to the evolution of public awareness and societal attitudes toward ADHD. The improved understanding of the neurological and genetic basis of ADHD has played a crucial role in diminishing stigma and fostering acceptance of the condition as a valid and controllable disorder. Efforts made by organizations like CHADD (Children and Adults with Attention-Deficit/Hyperactivity Disorder) and ADHD Europe have been instrumental in increasing awareness, providing support to individuals and families, and influencing policy changes to enhance the availability of diagnosis and treatment.

Ongoing research is currently investigating the potential benefits of mindfulness and physical exercise for individuals with ADHD. Research has demonstrated that engaging in mindfulness practices, such as meditation and yoga, can have positive effects on attention, emotional regulation, and overall well-being. In addition, there is evidence to suggest that engaging in regular physical exercise can lead to a decrease in symptoms of ADHD and an improvement in cognitive abilities. These comprehensive approaches provide additional strategies that can be incorporated into conventional treatment plans to offer a well-rounded approach to managing ADHD.

The latest research and findings have greatly enhanced our comprehension of ADHD, expanding it from a limited disorder to an intricate and diverse condition with various expressions and potential advantages. By incorporating the most up-to-date scientific findings and incorporating them into comprehensive treatment and support strategies, we can enhance our ability to assist individuals with ADHD in achieving their maximum potential. This evolving perspective not only empowers individuals with ADHD but also encourages society to recognize and appreciate the unique contributions that they can make. As research progresses, it offers the potential for significant advancements that can further improve the quality of life for individuals with ADHD and their families.

Environmental and Biological Elements

In order to gain a thorough understanding of ADHD (Attention Deficit Hyperactivity Disorder), it is necessary to conduct a comprehensive analysis of both environmental and biological factors. Through an examination of these factors, a deeper understanding can be gained regarding the complex dynamics that contribute to ADHD. This, in turn, can lead to the development of more effective interventions and supportive measures. The comprehensive perspective highlights that ADHD is a multifaceted condition, influenced by a variety of factors.

Understanding the nature of ADHD requires a clear understanding of the biological elements involved. Extensive research has provided substantial evidence regarding the genetic underpinnings of ADHD. Studies have shown that ADHD has a strong genetic component, with a substantial portion of the risk being attributed to genetic factors. Research findings from family and twin studies indicate that there is a higher likelihood for individuals to develop ADHD if they have a parent or sibling with the condition. Certain genes are closely involved in the regulation of neurotransmitters, including dopamine and norepinephrine, and their role is of utmost importance. The neurotransmitters play a crucial role in attention, impulse control, and executive function, all of which are commonly affected in individuals with ADHD.

Neuroimaging studies offer additional understanding of the biological foundations of ADHD. Methods such as functional magnetic resonance imaging (fMRI) and positron emission tomography (PET) scans have revealed disparities in brain structure and activity. As an example, the prefrontal cortex, a crucial region responsible for planning, decision-making, and regulating social behavior, frequently exhibits decreased activity in individuals diagnosed with ADHD. In addition, observations have been made regarding abnormalities in the basal ganglia and cerebellum, which are regions known for their involvement in motor control and cognitive function. The neurological differences discussed here provide insight into the behavioral manifestations of ADHD and highlight the condition's biological basis.

Prenatal and perinatal influences play a significant role in shaping the development of ADHD, along with genetic and neurological factors. Studies have indicated that the presence of specific environmental hazards during pregnancy, including tobacco smoke, alcohol, and illicit drugs, can elevate the probability of a child developing ADHD.

Maternal stress and inadequate prenatal nutrition are significant contributing factors. Environmental exposures have the potential to disrupt the typical development of the brain, resulting in the cognitive and behavioral symptoms that are commonly associated with ADHD. Birth complications, such as prematurity and low birth weight, additionally contribute to the risk, highlighting the significance of maternal health and prenatal care in reducing the development of ADHD.

The impact of postnatal environmental factors on the development and treatment of ADHD cannot be understated. Research has established a clear connection between early childhood adversity, such as exposure to violence, neglect, and socioeconomic hardship, and an elevated risk of ADHD. Highly demanding settings can negatively impact the development and functioning of the brain, which can worsen the symptoms associated with ADHD. In addition, the presence of environmental toxins, such as lead, can have a detrimental impact on cognitive development and behavior. Identifying these risk factors emphasizes the importance of implementing early interventions and creating supportive environments to minimize their effects.

The impact of diet and nutrition on ADHD should not be overlooked, as they play a crucial role in the environmental factors affecting this condition. Recent research indicates that the lack of specific nutrients, including omega-3 fatty acids, iron, zinc, and magnesium, may worsen symptoms associated with ADHD. Omega-3 fatty acids are crucial for maintaining optimal brain health and supporting its proper functioning. Research has indicated that the addition of these nutrients to one's diet can lead to a decrease in symptoms associated with ADHD and an enhancement in cognitive abilities. On the other hand, diets that contain high levels of sugar, artificial additives, and processed foods have been linked to higher levels of hyperactivity and inattention. Research in this area highlights the significance of maintaining a well-rounded diet to effectively manage symptoms of ADHD. It also provides evidence to support the integration of nutritional approaches into comprehensive treatment plans.

An essential aspect of comprehending ADHD lies in the examination of the interplay between genetic predisposition and environmental influences. Gene-environment interaction is a concept that explores how environmental factors can either worsen or alleviate the genetic susceptibility to ADHD. For instance, a child who has a genetic predisposition to ADHD may develop the condition when exposed to environmental stressors like family conflict or inadequate nutrition. On the other hand, creating a supportive environment that includes structured routines, positive reinforcement, and access to mental health resources can effectively manage and potentially decrease symptoms associated with ADHD. The interaction between genetic and environmental factors underscores the significance of individualized strategies for addressing and controlling ADHD.

A recent study on the epigenetic mechanisms involved in ADHD sheds light on the intricate relationship between genetics and the environment. Epigenetics encompasses modifications in gene expression that remain independent of the DNA sequence yet are susceptible to the impact of environmental factors. The observed alterations have the potential to impact the expression of genes linked to ADHD. This may provide an explanation as to why certain individuals with a genetic predisposition to ADHD manifest the condition while others do not. Having a clear understanding of these mechanisms provides opportunities for interventions that can potentially alter gene expression through environmental modifications, such as adopting a healthier diet, implementing effective stress management techniques, and utilizing targeted therapies.

Pharmacological treatments for ADHD typically prioritize the restoration of neurotransmitter levels to enhance attention and minimize impulsivity and hyperactivity. Stimulant medications, such as methylphenidate and amphetamines, are frequently prescribed and have demonstrated efficacy for a wide range of individuals. These medications have the ability to enhance neural communication and executive function by increasing dopamine and norepinephrine levels in the brain. Non-stimulant medications, such as atomoxetine and guanfacine, provide alternative options, especially for individuals who do not respond favorably to stimulants or encounter negative side effects. Continual research into these medications is focused on enhancing their effectiveness and minimizing potential risks, which will contribute to a more individualized approach to treating ADHD.

Behavioral therapies are a valuable addition to pharmacological treatments as they focus on the environmental and psychological factors associated with ADHD. Cognitive-behavioral therapy (CBT) assists individuals in enhancing coping strategies, refining organizational skills, and effectively managing impulsivity and emotional regulation. Parent training programs provide caregivers with valuable knowledge on effective strategies to support their children with ADHD. These strategies include positive reinforcement, consistent routines, and clear communication. These interventions have been shown to effectively reduce symptoms of ADHD and improve overall family functioning and quality of life. Recent technological advancements have greatly enhanced the accessibility of digital cognitive-behavioral therapy (CBT) programs and mobile applications. These innovative tools offer interactive and engaging platforms for individuals to effectively practice and reinforce the skills they have learned in therapy.

It is crucial to implement educational interventions to provide the necessary support for children with ADHD in academic settings. IEPs and 504 plans offer customized accommodations and modifications to address the specific requirements of students with ADHD. These plans may involve the extension of test times, the provision of preferred seating, and the utilization of assistive technology. Training teachers on ADHD can enhance classroom management and support strategies, resulting in a more inclusive and effective learning environment. Studies have shown that educational interventions have a positive impact on academic performance, behavior, self-esteem, and motivation in students with ADHD.

Occupational accommodations hold equal significance for adults diagnosed with ADHD. Implementing flexible work schedules, making task modifications, and utilizing organizational tools are effective strategies for managing ADHD symptoms in the workplace. Recognizing and addressing the specific strengths and challenges of employees with ADHD can result in higher productivity, job satisfaction, and improved workplace dynamics. Efforts made by organizations like CHADD (Children and Adults with Attention-Deficit/Hyperactivity Disorder) and ADHD Europe have played a crucial role in promoting supportive measures and reducing stigma, thereby fostering a more inclusive society.

To gain a comprehensive understanding of ADHD, it is essential to take into account various factors, including environmental and biological aspects. Through an examination of genetic, neurological, prenatal, and postnatal factors, as well as the influence of diet, nutrition, and stress, a comprehensive understanding of ADHD and its development can be achieved. Personalized interventions that address the unique needs of individuals with ADHD are crucial due to the interplay between genetic predisposition and environmental influences.

Progress in pharmacological treatments, behavioral therapies, educational and occupational accommodations, and advocacy efforts have all contributed to creating a more inclusive and supportive environment for individuals with ADHD. Through the utilization of these valuable insights and effective strategies, we have the ability to transform the obstacles commonly associated with ADHD into advantageous opportunities for achievement. This approach enables individuals with this condition to flourish in every facet of their lives.

CHAPTER 2

USING CHALLENGES TO BOOST YOUR ACHIEVEMENT

Overcoming Typical ADHD Challenges

Individuals with Attention Deficit Hyperactivity Disorder (ADHD) commonly encounter a range of difficulties that can have a significant impact on various areas of their lives, including academics, professional pursuits, personal relationships, and daily routines. Nevertheless, by adopting the appropriate mindset and employing effective strategies, these challenges can serve as potent drivers for personal development and success. By gaining a comprehensive understanding of the common challenges related to ADHD, individuals have the opportunity to leverage their distinct abilities and transform potential obstacles into valuable opportunities.

A common and significant obstacle faced by individuals with ADHD is the ability to sustain focus and attention. This challenge frequently arises in academic and professional environments where maintaining focused attention is essential. Tasks that demand extended cognitive exertion can be especially challenging. Recognizing the unique cognitive profile associated with ADHD enables the development of customized strategies to improve focus. Implementing strategies such as dividing tasks into smaller, more manageable portions and including regular intervals for rest can have a notable impact. In addition, utilizing tools such as timers and structured schedules can assist individuals in sustaining their focus over extended periods. By implementing these methods, individuals can effectively address the issue of inattention and utilize it as a platform for enhancing their organizational and time-management abilities.

Impulsivity is a characteristic commonly associated with ADHD, which can present difficulties in decision-making and social interactions. Impulsivity frequently leads to actions being taken without adequate forethought, resulting in challenges in both personal and professional relationships. Nevertheless, this characteristic can also be directed in a positive manner. For instance, individuals with ADHD often excel in environments that demand rapid thinking and adaptability. Professions in high-energy industries like emergency services, journalism, or entrepreneurship can be advantageous for individuals with ADHD due to their ability to thrive in spontaneous and dynamic environments. Developing mindfulness techniques and self-regulation strategies can be beneficial in managing impulsive behaviors, transforming them into valuable assets in situations that require quick responses.

Hyperactivity, often linked to ADHD, poses additional difficulties, especially in settings that require tranquility and composure. This characteristic may result in restlessness and challenges when engaging in sedentary tasks, which can pose difficulties in conventional classroom or office environments. Nevertheless, hyperactivity can be seen in a different light as a manifestation of high energy and enthusiasm. Engaging in physical activities like sports, dance, or any occupation that involves physical labor can effectively channel this abundant energy. In addition, integrating consistent physical exercise into daily routines can assist in managing hyperactivity, leading to enhanced focus and emotional regulation. Through directing their energy towards productive pursuits, individuals with ADHD have the potential to transform what may be perceived as a disruptive characteristic into a valuable source of energy and motivation.

Managing organizational tasks can be a common challenge for individuals with ADHD. Managing tasks, deadlines, and personal items can sometimes be a challenging endeavor. Nevertheless, these challenges may give rise to the creation of inventive organizational systems that are customized to meet specific requirements. Utilizing tools such as planners, digital apps, and reminder systems can be helpful in maintaining order. In addition, the use of visual aids such as color-coded calendars and lists can be beneficial for improving memory and task management. These adaptations not only assist in addressing the challenges of disorganization but also promote a proactive approach to managing responsibilities. Over time, individuals with ADHD can develop highly effective organizational skills that prove advantageous in both personal and professional domains.

Managing time effectively poses a significant challenge for individuals with ADHD. The perception of time in individuals with ADHD can be atypical, which can result in tendencies towards procrastination or a constant feeling of being behind schedule. One possible solution to this problem is to implement strategies that improve time awareness and management. Methods such as utilizing alarms, establishing timers for tasks, and dividing projects into smaller steps with specific deadlines can yield significant results. In addition, it is important to prioritize tasks and concentrate on high-impact activities in order to enhance productivity and meet important deadlines. By honing these time-management skills, individuals with ADHD have the opportunity to turn a potential weakness into a strength, thereby improving their efficiency and dependability.

Individuals with ADHD commonly experience difficulties in emotional regulation, resulting in increased sensitivity and challenges in stress management. These strong emotions can lead to feelings of frustration, anxiety, or fluctuations in mood. Nevertheless, developing emotional awareness can be transformed into a valuable advantage. Practices such as mindfulness meditation, cognitive-behavioral therapy (CBT), and regular physical activity have been shown to be effective in regulating emotions and reducing stress. These techniques have the potential to enhance emotional stability and improve empathy and interpersonal skills. People with ADHD frequently demonstrate a notable level of emotional intelligence, which can be utilized to cultivate robust and meaningful connections and thrive in positions that demand empathy and comprehension.

Individuals with ADHD often face challenges in social interactions due to their impulsivity, hyperactivity, and difficulties with attention. These factors can make it difficult for them to navigate social situations and maintain meaningful connections with others. These characteristics can occasionally result in miscommunications or tense interpersonal dynamics. Nevertheless, individuals with ADHD frequently possess a distinct charm and enthusiasm that can be highly captivating. Improving social interactions and building lasting relationships can be achieved through the development of active listening skills and the practice of social cues. Support groups and social skills training offer valuable opportunities for individuals to practice these skills in a supportive environment. Overcoming social challenges can lead to the development of strong interpersonal skills and a robust support network.

Students with ADHD often face distinct challenges in the academic environment. Some individuals' learning styles may not be well-suited to traditional teaching methods and classroom settings. Recognizing these challenges can lead to the development of personalized learning strategies that take advantage of the strengths of ADHD. Utilizing methods such as hands-on learning, interactive lessons, and the integration of technology can effectively enhance engagement and comprehension. In order to facilitate academic success, it is important to provide accommodations such as extended time for tests, preferential seating, and tailored assignments. By advocating for their needs and making use of the resources at their disposal, students with ADHD have the potential to excel academically.

Individuals with ADHD may face difficulties in the workplace, such as task completion, organization, and maintaining focus. Nevertheless, numerous employers acknowledge the distinct strengths that individuals with ADHD can offer, including their creativity, problem-solving skills, and exceptional energy levels. Individuals with ADHD can achieve professional success by pursuing roles that align with their strengths and interests. Engaging in transparent dialogue with employers regarding specific needs and accommodations can foster a more nurturing work environment. Having a flexible schedule, a variety of tasks, and a structured workspace can significantly improve productivity and job satisfaction. Recognizing and harnessing the distinct strengths of individuals with ADHD enables them to excel in their professional endeavors and make substantial impacts in their respective domains.

To address the common difficulties associated with ADHD,

it is necessary to employ a combination of self-awareness, strategic planning, and utilizing the resources at hand. Receiving support from family, friends, and professionals is essential in this process. Establishing a robust support network is crucial for individuals with ADHD, as it offers the necessary encouragement and assistance to effectively navigate their challenges. Therapy, coaching, and support groups provide valuable guidance and strategies for effectively managing symptoms and enhancing overall well-being.

ADHD poses a range of challenges, but with the right approach, these difficulties can be turned into chances for personal development and success. By gaining a comprehensive understanding of the distinct characteristics associated with ADHD, individuals can effectively develop strategies to overcome challenges and leverage their inherent strengths. This process utilizes a thorough approach, incorporating tailored strategies, conducive environments, and self-reflection.

By redefining ADHD as a distinct cognitive profile rather than a disorder, individuals have the opportunity to tap into their full potential and accomplish remarkable achievements. The process of transforming obstacles into accomplishments not only empowers individuals with ADHD but also enhances the wider community by highlighting the varied talents and perspectives that ADHD individuals contribute.

Tales of Revival and Success

Stories of revival and success frequently act as compelling evidence of the human spirit's capacity to conquer adversity and turn challenges into victories. These stories provide a profound reflection on the experiences of individuals with ADHD, showcasing their ability to overcome challenges and achieve remarkable success. By acquiring a deep understanding of and fully embracing their distinct cognitive profiles, individuals with ADHD have the ability to transform challenges into valuable opportunities. They can harness their experiences to drive significant personal and professional development.

Attention Deficit Hyperactivity Disorder, commonly known as ADHD, poses a range of challenges, such as issues with attention, impulsivity, and hyperactivity. These characteristics may present challenges in various academic, social, and professional environments. Nevertheless, with determination and effective leadership, numerous individuals with ADHD have not only learned to adapt but have also excelled, transforming their perceived challenges into unique strengths. These stories showcase the remarkable potential that lies within individuals to leverage their distinct talents and attain remarkable success, even in the face of adversity.

An interesting illustration is that of Richard Branson, the

founder of the Virgin Group. Branson encountered considerable academic difficulties during his school years due to his diagnosis of ADHD and dyslexia. Conventional education systems frequently did not cater to his preferred learning style, resulting in difficulties for him to stay on track. Nevertheless, Branson's entrepreneurial spirit and innovative thinking, traits often linked to ADHD, allowed him to identify opportunities that went unnoticed by others. His exceptional problem-solving skills and unwavering determination resulted in the establishment of a highly renowned international brand. Branson's story exemplifies how ADHD can be seen as a catalyst for creativity and entrepreneurial success.

Moreover, the story of Simone Biles, an esteemed Olympic gold medalist, highlights the remarkable ability of individuals with ADHD to thrive in demanding circumstances. Biles, who has been transparent regarding her ADHD diagnosis, has encountered examination and prejudice throughout her career. Despite the numerous challenges she has faced, she has achieved an exceptional level of success and is widely recognized as one of the most accomplished gymnasts in history. Her success can be attributed to both her physical abilities and her mental resilience and determination. Biles's journey underscores the significance of persistence and advocating for oneself in attaining success, showcasing how ADHD can serve as a catalyst for personal growth rather than a hindrance.

Dr. Ned Hallowell's story is truly inspiring, especially within the academic community. Dr. Hallowell, a renowned psychiatrist and accomplished author, received a diagnosis of ADHD in adulthood. Throughout his life, he encountered the common challenges associated with ADHD, such as issues with organization and concentration. Nevertheless, Hallowell utilized his personal experiences to drive his dedication towards assisting individuals with ADHD. With his extensive knowledge and experience, he has emerged as a prominent figure in the field. He has authored numerous highly acclaimed books on the subject and established the Hallowell Centers, renowned for their holistic approach to offering comprehensive support to individuals with ADHD and related conditions. Hallowell's career demonstrates the positive outcomes that can arise from acknowledging and embracing one's ADHD. It serves as a testament to how this understanding can contribute to a rewarding and influential professional journey.

The realm of entertainment is replete with numerous instances of individuals who have effectively utilized their ADHD to attain noteworthy accomplishments. Jim Carrey, the renowned actor and comedian, has openly discussed his experience with ADHD, showcasing his dynamic performances and exceptional improvisational abilities. Carrey's exceptional energy and creativity, qualities frequently associated with ADHD, have distinguished him as a remarkable figure in his industry. His capacity to focus his energy on his work has resulted in a remarkably accomplished profession in Hollywood. The story of Carrey illustrates how individuals with ADHD can leverage their unique characteristics to thrive in creative and dynamic fields.

These stories of resurgence and achievement highlight a recurring motif: the skill to transform obstacles into advantageous situations. People diagnosed with ADHD often have distinct strengths, including creativity, resilience, and the ability to think divergently. By prioritizing these strengths and implementing effective strategies to address their challenges, individuals can attain remarkable levels of success. This process entails a blend of personal introspection, assistance, and methodical strategizing.

Having a clear understanding of oneself is an essential initial step in embarking on this journey. Gaining a comprehensive understanding of ADHD and its impact on different areas of life empowers individuals to devise tailored approaches for effectively managing their symptoms. One possible approach is to utilize methods that can enhance concentration, such as dividing tasks into smaller, more manageable steps or employing visual aids. Additionally, there are various strategies available for effectively managing impulsiveness, such as practicing mindfulness and utilizing self-regulation techniques. By gaining an understanding of their distinct cognitive profiles, individuals with ADHD can utilize their strengths and address their weaknesses.

Receiving support from family, friends, and professionals is crucial in this process. An effective support network can offer motivation, valuable resources, and practical aid. Therapists and ADHD coaches can provide valuable guidance on effective strategies for managing symptoms, while supportive family members and friends can contribute to creating an environment that fosters success. This network offers valuable assistance and also plays a role in alleviating the stigma and isolation that individuals with ADHD may face.

Strategic planning is a crucial element in transforming ADHD challenges into accomplishments. To effectively achieve desired outcomes, it is essential to establish attainable objectives, implement well-organized schedules, and leverage appropriate tools and technologies to optimize efficiency. For example, utilizing digital planners and reminder apps can assist individuals in maintaining organization and staying focused on their tasks. In addition, individuals can enhance their chances of achieving success and finding fulfillment by actively seeking out environments that are in line with their strengths. As an illustration, individuals who possess high energy levels tend to flourish in dynamic and fast-paced work environments, whereas those with creative talents often excel in artistic or entrepreneurial pursuits.

Richard Branson, Simone Biles, Dr. Ned Hallowell, and Jim

Carrey exemplify the various paths to success that individuals with ADHD can pursue. Every one of these individuals encountered substantial obstacles, yet they utilized their distinct capabilities to triumph over them. The achievements of individuals with ADHD are often attributed to the unique qualities associated with this condition rather than in spite of it. These individuals' experiences serve as strong reminders that ADHD, despite its challenges, also presents distinct strengths that can be utilized to achieve exceptional results.

The stories of individuals with ADHD who have experienced revival and achieved success serve as a powerful reminder of the transformative potential that can arise from overcoming challenges. By gaining a comprehensive understanding of their distinct cognitive profiles, individuals with ADHD can effectively implement strategies to effectively manage their symptoms and capitalize on their inherent strengths. Self-awareness, support, and strategic planning are crucial elements in this process, empowering individuals to attain personal and professional success.

These stories exemplify resilience and innovation, showcasing how individuals with ADHD can achieve extraordinary accomplishments. By emphasizing their strengths and employing innovative problem-solving techniques, individuals with ADHD have the potential to transform their challenges into opportunities for personal growth and achievement, positively impacting both their own lives and the lives of those in their community.

CHAPTER 3

TECHNIQUES FOR DAY-TO-DAY ACHIEVEMENT

Practical Tips for Daily Management

Effectively managing ADHD requires the integration of practical strategies into daily routines to improve focus, organization, and overall productivity. Mastering these techniques is crucial for turning the obstacles of ADHD into chances for success. Through the implementation of customized strategies that are in line with the distinct cognitive profiles of individuals diagnosed with ADHD, it is feasible to alleviate prevalent symptoms and cultivate a more organized and satisfying lifestyle.

Establishing a consistent routine is a fundamental aspect of daily management for individuals with ADHD. Consistency aids in establishing a feeling of predictability and authority, which can be especially advantageous for individuals facing challenges with time management and organization. It is important to establish a well-organized schedule that covers various aspects of your daily routine, such as waking up, meal times, work or school activities, exercise, and relaxation. Following a regular schedule can help individuals avoid feeling overwhelmed by unstructured time and enhance their ability to concentrate on specific tasks.

Integrating physical activity into one's daily routine is a practical strategy that can greatly benefit individuals with ADHD. Research has demonstrated that exercise can effectively improve concentration, decrease impulsivity, and enhance mood, all of which play a crucial role in managing symptoms associated with ADHD. Engaging in regular physical activity has been found to have a positive impact on the production of neurotransmitters like dopamine and norepinephrine. These neurotransmitters are known to play important roles in attention and executive function. Participating in activities such as running, swimming, or yoga can effectively channel surplus energy and enhance mental clarity.

Mindfulness and meditation practices have been found to provide significant benefits for individuals managing ADHD on a daily basis. These techniques promote the cultivation of heightened self-awareness regarding thoughts, emotions, and physical sensations, fostering a state of tranquility and concentration. Incorporating mindfulness exercises into your daily routine, such as deep breathing, progressive muscle relaxation, or guided meditation, can effectively aid in stress management and enhance attention. Regular practice of mindfulness can improve individuals' ability to stay focused and attentive, leading to a decrease in distractions and impulsive behaviors.

Efficient time management is a vital aspect of effectively

managing ADHD on a daily basis. People diagnosed with ADHD frequently experience difficulties in accurately perceiving time, which can make it challenging for them to effectively prioritize tasks and meet deadlines. By incorporating tools like planners, calendars, and digital reminders, individuals can develop a clear visual representation of their tasks and deadlines, enabling them to effectively manage their time. By dividing tasks into smaller, more manageable steps and assigning specific time limits to each step, individuals can avoid feeling overwhelmed and instead experience a sense of accomplishment.

Establishing a well-structured and undisturbed setting is crucial for optimizing efficiency and concentration. It is recommended that individuals with ADHD consider decluttering their physical space by keeping only essential items within reach. This practice can prove to be beneficial for them. Creating specific zones for various activities, such as work, study, and relaxation, can effectively establish boundaries and minimize potential distractions. In addition, utilizing noise-canceling headphones or playing background music can help reduce auditory distractions and promote focused attention.

Technology can be a valuable tool for effectively managing ADHD on a daily basis. There are numerous applications and software programs available that can be utilized to enhance organization, time management, and concentration. Task management apps such as Todoist or Trello can assist individuals in tracking their tasks and deadlines. Similarly, focus-enhancing apps like Forest or Focus@Will offer tools to minimize distractions and sustain concentration. Through the utilization of digital resources, individuals with ADHD can enhance their daily routines and optimize their overall efficiency.

Considering the nutritional aspects is crucial when it comes to effectively managing ADHD on a daily basis. A well-rounded diet that incorporates a diverse range of nutrients has the potential to enhance cognitive function and mood. Including foods that are high in protein, omega-3 fatty acids, and complex carbohydrates in your diet can contribute to the stabilization of energy levels and the promotion of brain health. It is crucial to refrain from consuming excessive amounts of sugar and processed foods, as they can lead to fluctuations in energy levels and hinder focus. Ensuring adequate hydration by consuming an ample amount of water throughout the day can additionally enhance cognitive function and promote overall well-being.

Establishing good sleep habits is essential for effectively managing the symptoms of ADHD. Inadequate sleep can worsen problems related to attention, impulsivity, and emotional regulation. To improve the quality of your sleep, it is important to establish a consistent sleep schedule, create a relaxing bedtime routine, and ensure a comfortable sleep environment. It is recommended to refrain from consuming caffeine and using electronic devices before going to bed in order to enhance the quality of sleep. By emphasizing the importance of maintaining healthy sleep habits, individuals with ADHD can enhance their cognitive function and daily performance.

One practical suggestion for effectively managing ADHD on a daily basis is to actively seek and make use of social support. Establishing connections with friends, family members, or support groups can offer valuable encouragement and accountability. Exchanging experiences and strategies with individuals who have a deep understanding of the challenges posed by ADHD can provide a sense of connection and empowerment, reducing feelings of isolation and assisting in the effective management of symptoms. In addition, individuals may benefit from seeking assistance from professionals such as therapists, coaches, or counselors who can provide personalized guidance and effective strategies for managing ADHD.

It is crucial to cultivate robust self-advocacy skills for effective daily management of ADHD. It is important for individuals with ADHD to assert themselves and express their needs in different environments, including educational and professional settings. One possible approach is to consider requesting additional time for tasks, utilizing assistive technologies, or establishing a more structured work environment. By advocating for their needs, individuals with ADHD can work towards creating environments that are more supportive and accommodating, ultimately facilitating their success.

Developing resilience and cultivating a positive mindset are crucial for effectively navigating the daily challenges associated with ADHD. Acknowledging and commemorating minor accomplishments can enhance one's self-confidence and drive. Adopting a growth mindset can be beneficial for individuals with ADHD, as it allows them to perceive challenges as chances for personal development and progress. This mindset shift enables them to approach their daily tasks with a positive and proactive attitude. Resilience can be enhanced by engaging in regular self-reflection, recognizing individual strengths, and establishing practical and achievable objectives.

It can be advantageous to include regular check-ins and self-assessments as part of the daily routine. It is important for individuals with ADHD to engage in self-reflection to evaluate the effectiveness of their strategies and identify areas that require improvement. This process allows for necessary adjustments to be made, ensuring that they can stay on track and achieve their goals. One possible approach is to engage in activities such as journaling, utilizing self-assessment tools, or seeking feedback from a trusted friend or professional to monitor and evaluate progress. It is important for individuals to regularly assess themselves in order to maintain awareness of their progress and to develop effective strategies for managing their ADHD symptoms.

In order to effectively manage ADHD on a daily basis, it is crucial to adopt a comprehensive and individualized approach. By implementing effective strategies such as establishing consistent routines, incorporating regular physical activity, practicing mindfulness, and utilizing technology, individuals with ADHD can improve their ability to concentrate, stay organized, and increase productivity. Emphasizing the importance of maintaining good sleep hygiene, considering nutritional factors, and seeking social support can greatly enhance daily management. Developing resilience, honing self-advocacy skills, and consistently evaluating progress are essential elements of an effective ADHD management plan.

By implementing these practical tips and strategies, individuals with ADHD can enhance their daily functioning and transform their obstacles into chances for success. This approach takes into account the specific symptoms of ADHD and aims to promote a sense of empowerment and confidence. Individuals with ADHD can achieve their full potential and lead fulfilling and successful lives with the appropriate tools and support.

Techniques for Managing Time and Organizing

Effective time management and organizational skills are crucial for attaining daily success, particularly for individuals with ADHD. The challenges linked to ADHD, such as problems sustaining attention, controlling impulses, and organizing tasks, can make these skills particularly difficult to attain. By implementing precise methods and tactics, individuals can overcome these challenges and turn their daily routines into well-organized and fruitful pursuits.

Utilizing planners and scheduling tools is a highly effective method for time management. These tools offer a clear and objective way to visually represent tasks and deadlines, enabling individuals to effectively prioritize their responsibilities and allocate their time. Digital planners, such as those found on smartphones and computers, provide the added advantage of setting reminders and alerts, which can be essential for individuals who face challenges with time management. By breaking down tasks into smaller, more manageable steps and allocating specific time slots for each activity, individuals can prevent feelings of overwhelm and maintain a clear focus on their goals.

Furthermore, incorporating the Pomodoro Technique into your time management strategy can greatly improve productivity. This approach utilizes brief, concentrated intervals, usually lasting 25 minutes, followed by a five-minute pause. Following the completion of four intervals, a longer break is taken. This technique utilizes the brain's capacity to concentrate intensely for brief periods, making it especially effective for individuals with ADHD who may struggle with sustained focus. The Pomodoro Technique is effective in sustaining productivity and preventing burnout by incorporating regular breaks.

Creating a daily routine is a crucial method for effectively managing time and maintaining organization. Having a consistent routine can offer structure and predictability, which can be particularly advantageous for individuals with ADHD. It is recommended to establish a consistent schedule that includes specific times for waking up, meals, work or study sessions, exercise, and relaxation. By adhering to a consistent schedule, individuals can alleviate the cognitive burden of determining their next course of action and mitigate potential distractions. Having a well-organized routine can also help foster the formation of positive habits, which in turn can have a positive impact on one's overall well-being and productivity.

Establishing a dedicated workspace is essential for ensuring efficiency and concentration. An uncluttered and well-organized workspace can greatly minimize distractions and improve focus. It is important for individuals to ensure that their workspace is properly equipped with all the necessary materials and tools. This will help minimize the need to search for items and avoid interruptions to their workflow. In order to optimize concentration on tasks, it is advisable to reduce visual and auditory disturbances. This can be achieved by utilizing noise-canceling headphones or by positioning oneself away from windows.

Utilizing organizational tools, such as to-do lists and task management apps, can also yield significant results. To-do lists are a valuable tool for individuals to effectively manage their tasks and responsibilities. They provide a concise and organized overview of what needs to be accomplished, ensuring that nothing falls through the cracks. By organizing tasks based on their level of importance and urgency, one can effectively address critical activities in a timely manner. Task management applications, such as Todoist or Trello, provide a range of useful features, including categorization, deadlines, and progress tracking. These features can greatly assist in maintaining organization and effectively managing responsibilities.

Another effective technique for time management and task organization is setting SMART goals. SMART stands for Specific, Measurable, Achievable, Relevant, and Time-bound. By following this approach, individuals can enhance their productivity and ensure that their goals are well-defined and attainable within a specific timeframe. Setting SMART goals can provide a clear direction and a sense of purpose, which can help individuals stay focused and motivated. As an illustration, instead of establishing an ambiguous objective such as "study more," a SMART goal would entail dedicating one hour each day this week to studying biology chapters 3 and 4. This level of detail allows individuals with ADHD to effectively break down their goals into manageable tasks and monitor their advancement over a period of time.

Time blocking is an effective strategy that entails allocating dedicated time blocks for various tasks or activities throughout the day. By allocating designated time slots to specific tasks, individuals can ensure that each activity receives undivided attention and is not inadvertently neglected. Implementing time blocking can assist in establishing a well-rounded schedule that incorporates dedicated time for work, leisure, and personal pursuits, thereby fostering a more harmonious work-life equilibrium. This approach is highly effective in handling extensive projects or multiple responsibilities, as it ensures that tasks do not accumulate and become overwhelming.

Furthermore, it is crucial to acknowledge the significance of self-awareness in effectively managing time and maintaining organization. Gaining insight into one's personal strengths and weaknesses can be instrumental in developing customized strategies that are most effective for individuals. For instance, certain individuals may discover that they experience higher levels of productivity at specific times of the day, enabling them to effectively plan and tackle their most challenging tasks during these periods. Some individuals may find it beneficial to incorporate regular breaks into their routines in order to maintain focus.

Self-compassion and flexibility are crucial factors in effective time management. People with ADHD may face obstacles and difficulties, and it is important to approach these situations with empathy and understanding. Adhering strictly to schedules and goals can result in feelings of frustration and exhaustion. Instead, it is important to make adjustments and acknowledge that achieving perfection is not the primary objective. This approach can contribute to maintaining a positive and productive mindset. Being able to adapt plans without feeling discouraged by unexpected changes or obstacles is important for individuals. Flexibility allows for adjustments to be made as needed.

Receiving support from family, friends, and colleagues can be crucial to effectively managing time and maintaining organization. When individuals share their goals and responsibilities with a supportive network, they can benefit from increased accountability and encouragement. One way to boost motivation and meet deadlines is by engaging in study groups or collaborating with colleagues on projects. In addition, it can be beneficial to seek guidance from professionals who specialize in ADHD, such as coaches or therapists. They can offer valuable insights and personalized strategies to improve time management and organization.

Integrating self-care practices into daily routines is an essential aspect of sustaining productivity and organization. Engaging in regular exercise, getting sufficient sleep, and maintaining a healthy diet all play a crucial role in enhancing cognitive function and boosting energy levels. These factors are vital for effectively managing one's time. Engaging in mindfulness practices, such as meditation and deep breathing exercises, can effectively alleviate stress and enhance concentration. This, in turn, facilitates better organization and task management.

In addition, technology provides a wide range of tools and resources that can assist in enhancing time management and organization. Applications specifically developed for managing ADHD, such as Forest for enhancing focus or Habitica for tracking habits, offer creative solutions to frequently encountered difficulties. By incorporating these technologies, daily routines can be optimized, and productivity can be improved. These tools offer features such as reminders, progress tracking, and rewards for task completion, which can greatly enhance efficiency.

In order to achieve successful time management and

organization, it is crucial to engage in continuous reflection and make necessary adjustments. Consistently evaluating goals, routines, and strategies enables individuals to pinpoint areas of success and areas that require enhancement. Regularly engaging in reflective practice is crucial to ensuring that techniques remain effective and aligned with changing needs and priorities. By incorporating these reflections into our routine, we can consistently improve our time management and organizational skills, fostering ongoing personal growth and development.

Effective time management and organizational skills are essential for daily success, especially for individuals with ADHD. Enhancing productivity and reducing challenges associated with ADHD can be achieved through the implementation of practical techniques. These techniques include using planners, establishing routines, creating designated workspaces, and setting SMART goals. In order to enhance time management and organization, it is important to cultivate self-awareness, flexibility, and self-compassion.

Additionally, utilizing support networks and technology can also be beneficial. By engaging in regular self-reflection and making necessary adjustments, individuals can consistently improve their strategies, resulting in long-term success and satisfaction in their everyday lives. By implementing these comprehensive strategies, individuals with ADHD can transform their distinct challenges into opportunities for success, thereby creating a more structured and fruitful future.

CHAPTER 4

ESTABLISHING A SUPPORT NETWORK

Navigating Relationships and Social Dynamics

Understanding and managing relationships and social dynamics is an essential component in building a strong support network, especially for individuals with ADHD. Establishing and sustaining positive relationships can pose difficulties as a result of the symptoms commonly associated with ADHD, including impulsivity, inattention, and challenges with emotional regulation. Nevertheless, by implementing effective strategies and gaining a comprehensive understanding, individuals with ADHD can develop significant relationships that offer emotional support, practical assistance, and a sense of belonging.

To effectively navigate relationships, it is crucial to have a clear understanding of how ADHD impacts social interactions. Conversations can pose challenges for individuals with ADHD, as maintaining focus may be difficult. This can result in misunderstandings or a sense of disconnection. In addition, the tendency to act impulsively can lead to speaking out of turn or interrupting others, potentially causing strain in relationships. Understanding these patterns is crucial for devising tactics to minimize their influence.

Efficient and effective communication plays a crucial role in fostering strong and harmonious relationships. Individuals with ADHD are advised to approach interactions with greater mindfulness and intentionality. Developing active listening skills is highly valuable, as it requires complete focus on the speaker's words instead of formulating a response. Methods such as maintaining eye contact, nodding, and offering verbal affirmations can effectively showcase engagement and foster rapport. Paraphrasing the other person's words can be beneficial in promoting comprehension and acknowledging the receipt of their message.

One crucial element of effective communication is the ability to control impulsivity during conversations. One way to accomplish this is by implementing self-regulation techniques, such as taking a moment to pause before responding and carefully considering the potential consequences of our words before speaking. Establishing a practice of pausing and reflecting before responding can effectively minimize impulsive comments and promote more considerate exchanges. Through the implementation of these strategies, individuals diagnosed with ADHD can enhance their communication abilities and cultivate more robust and mutually respectful relationships.

Having a thorough grasp of emotions and effectively handling them is essential for successfully navigating social dynamics. Individuals with ADHD frequently experience heightened emotional sensitivity, resulting in strong reactions during social interactions. Enhancing relationship skills can be greatly achieved through the development of emotional intelligence. This involves the ability to recognize, understand, and manage one's emotions. Methods such as mindfulness and cognitive-behavioral strategies can assist individuals with ADHD in enhancing their emotional awareness and cultivating healthier coping mechanisms for managing stress and frustration.

Setting clear boundaries is a crucial aspect of maintaining healthy relationships. Establishing boundaries is crucial in interpersonal interactions, as they provide clarity and prevent any potential misunderstandings or resentments between individuals. Individuals with ADHD may find it helpful to carefully consider and plan how they communicate their boundaries. It is beneficial to pinpoint particular areas where boundaries are necessary, such as managing time, respecting personal space, or understanding communication preferences. Identifying these areas is crucial in order to establish effective communication boundaries with friends, family members, and colleagues. By clearly and respectfully communicating these boundaries, conflicts can be avoided and mutual respect can be fostered.

Developing a support network also entails actively seeking and cultivating relationships with individuals who are empathetic and encouraging towards ADHD. These relationships offer a secure environment for discussing challenges, exchanging experiences, and receiving support. Connecting with others who have ADHD, whether through support groups or online communities, can be advantageous. These individuals can provide valuable insights and empathy due to their shared experiences. Involving trusted friends and family members in the journey of managing ADHD can enhance relationships and foster a supportive environment.

Having access to professional support is an essential

component of a robust support network. Professionals who specialize in ADHD can offer valuable guidance and strategies for managing symptoms and enhancing social skills. Interacting with experts provides a formal and organized environment to tackle specific relationship issues and create customized strategies for navigating social dynamics. By integrating professional assistance into their network, individuals with ADHD can improve their overall well-being and success in relationships.

Individuals with ADHD often encounter unique challenges and opportunities when it comes to navigating romantic relationships. In order to maintain a healthy romantic relationship, it is essential to prioritize open communication, mutual understanding, and shared effort. Both partners should prioritize educating themselves about ADHD and its impact on their relationship. Developing this understanding can promote empathy and minimize potential conflicts that may arise from misinterpretations of ADHD symptoms.

Engaging in couples therapy can prove to be a highly effective method for addressing specific concerns and devising strategies to improve communication, intimacy, and partnership.

ADHD can have a significant impact on interactions and relationships within the context of family dynamics. Parents who have ADHD may face difficulties in effectively balancing household responsibilities while also maintaining a strong bond with their children. On the other hand, children with ADHD may benefit from receiving extra support and understanding from their parents. Establishing consistent routines and structures that address the specific needs associated with ADHD can contribute to fostering a harmonious and supportive home environment. Engaging in open discussions about ADHD within the family can foster better comprehension and collaboration among its members.

Friendships are an important component of a support

network. Companionship, support, and a sense of belonging are some of the benefits that friends offer. Individuals with ADHD may face challenges maintaining friendships due to difficulties with consistency and follow-through. Implementing strategies such as scheduling regular check-ins, setting reminders for social engagements, and openly discussing challenges related to ADHD can contribute to the maintenance of friendships. By placing a strong emphasis on reliability and effective communication, individuals with ADHD have the ability to cultivate enduring and significant friendships.

Establishing workplace relationships is crucial for creating a comprehensive support network. Attention Deficit Hyperactivity Disorder (ADHD) can have a significant impact on professional interactions and performance. It is crucial to develop effective strategies for managing these challenges. Establishing open lines of communication with supervisors and colleagues regarding ADHD can contribute to the development of a supportive work environment. Seeking appropriate accommodations, such as adjustments to work hours or a conducive work environment, can enhance the performance of individuals with ADHD. Developing strong professional relationships with colleagues through collaborative efforts and mutual support can significantly contribute to increased job satisfaction and career advancement.

Students with ADHD may encounter distinct social difficulties in educational environments. Establishing strong connections with teachers, peers, and school counselors can create a supportive foundation for achieving academic success. Teachers who have knowledge of a student's ADHD can provide customized assistance and adjustments, such as granting additional time for assignments or offering alternative evaluation methods. Peer support groups and mentoring programs offer significant benefits for students with ADHD, including valuable social connections and academic assistance.

Understanding and successfully navigating social dynamics requires a constant commitment to learning, adapting, and personal growth. One must possess qualities such as patience, empathy, and a dedication to personal growth. Through the deliberate cultivation of effective communication skills, emotional regulation, and the establishment of clear boundaries, individuals diagnosed with ADHD have the potential to develop more robust and gratifying interpersonal connections. Developing strong and empathetic relationships, both in personal and professional spheres, can greatly contribute to success in different social environments.

Developing a strong support network by effectively navigating relationships and social dynamics is crucial for individuals with ADHD. Through a comprehensive understanding of how ADHD impacts social interactions, the implementation of effective communication techniques, the management of emotions, and the establishment of clear boundaries, individuals can successfully cultivate and sustain healthy relationships.

Building a comprehensive support network involves actively participating in supportive communities, seeking guidance from professionals, and promoting understanding in various contexts, such as romantic relationships, family dynamics, friendships, and the workplace. By consistently applying effort and maintaining self-awareness, individuals with ADHD have the ability to transform their challenges into opportunities for social success and overall well-being.

Finding and Utilizing Support Networks

It is essential for individuals facing a range of challenges, including those associated with ADHD, to establish a support network. Discovering and utilizing support networks entails recognizing and engaging with various sources of assistance, such as friends, family, professionals, or communities, to receive emotional, practical, and informational support. These networks are crucial in assisting individuals in navigating the intricacies of everyday life, effectively managing symptoms, and attaining their objectives.

An essential source of support for individuals with ADHD is their immediate family. Family members play a vital role in providing unwavering love, empathy, and motivation, serving as an essential source of emotional support. Individuals with ADHD can find solace and support from loved ones who possess a deep understanding of the unique challenges they face. This understanding can foster empathy and validation, ultimately reducing feelings of isolation. In addition, family members can provide practical assistance by helping to organize schedules, offering reminders, and providing transportation to appointments. This can help alleviate daily responsibilities and make things more manageable.

In addition to immediate family, extended family members can also play a crucial role in offering support. Extended family members can provide valuable insights, guidance, and support. They can offer a wider support network that enhances the support provided by immediate family members. This additional network brings diverse perspectives and experiences, enriching the individual's overall support system.

Having a strong support network is crucial for individuals with ADHD, and friends play a vital role in this network. Having close friends who are knowledgeable about and accepting of the challenges associated with ADHD can provide valuable companionship, empathy, and a strong sense of belonging. These friendships offer chances for socializing, engaging in recreational activities, and finding relaxation, all of which contribute to one's overall well-being and quality of life. Individuals can benefit from having friends who can serve as accountability partners, providing support and encouragement to help them stay focused on their goals and commitments.

Experts in ADHD, such as therapists, coaches, and counselors, are highly valuable resources for individuals seeking support. These professionals are highly skilled in providing personalized guidance, strategies, and interventions to assist individuals in effectively managing symptoms and enhancing their overall quality of life. Therapists provide emotional support, assist individuals in developing coping strategies, and address underlying issues such as anxiety or depression. Coaches offer valuable support in areas such as goal-setting, time management, and organizational skills, enabling individuals to reach their maximum potential.

Within educational settings, teachers, counselors, and other school personnel possess the expertise to provide valuable support to students diagnosed with ADHD. Teachers who possess expertise in ADHD can offer accommodations, modifications, and supplementary support to facilitate academic success for students. School counselors are equipped to provide students with emotional support, guidance, and access to necessary resources to help them navigate challenges and access the services they need. Peer support groups and mentoring programs can be beneficial resources for students with ADHD, offering valuable connections and assistance.

Workplaces can play a crucial role in providing support for individuals with ADHD. Employers who have a comprehensive understanding of and make accommodations for challenges related to ADHD can foster a work environment that is supportive, encouraging success and well-being. Some potential solutions could involve implementing flexible work schedules, providing remote work options, or offering accommodations like noise-canceling headphones or ergonomic workstations. Being aware of an individual's ADHD can enable colleagues to provide understanding, assistance, and encouragement, fostering a positive and inclusive workplace culture.

Online communities and support groups are highly beneficial for individuals with ADHD, providing them with valuable support and fostering connections. These communities offer a platform for individuals to share their experiences, exchange advice, and receive validation from others who have a deep understanding of the challenges associated with living with ADHD. Online forums, social media groups, and virtual support meetings provide convenient avenues for individuals to connect with others who share similar interests and gain access to valuable resources and information.

Discovering and utilizing support networks typically necessitates a proactive approach and a willingness to actively seek assistance. One possible approach is to consider reaching out to friends or family members for assistance. Another option is to seek referrals to professionals who have expertise in ADHD. Additionally, joining support groups or community organizations can provide valuable resources and support. It is crucial for individuals to assert their needs, engage in open communication about their challenges, and be open to the support provided by others.

Once support networks are in place, it is crucial to make the most of them. Regularly checking in with supportive friends or family members, attending therapy or coaching sessions, or actively participating in support group meetings may be beneficial in maintaining a healthy support system. People can also contribute to their support networks by providing assistance to others who are facing similar challenges. This creates a reciprocal relationship that promotes mutual growth and empowerment.

Establishing and utilizing support networks is crucial for

individuals with ADHD to effectively manage symptoms, navigate challenges, and achieve their goals. These networks offer support in the form of emotions, practical assistance, and information from a range of sources, such as family, friends, professionals, and communities. Through proactive efforts to seek support, maintain open communication with others, and engage in support networks, individuals with ADHD can develop resilience, improve their well-being, and achieve success in all areas of their lives.

CHAPTER 5

SUCCESS IN THE WORKPLACE AND SCHOOL

Techniques for Success in the Workplace

Achieving success in the workplace is a complex undertaking that necessitates a blend of various skills, strategies, and attitudes. Individuals with ADHD often face distinct challenges when it comes to managing their time, staying organized, communicating effectively, and maintaining focus in the workplace. Individuals with ADHD can improve their performance, productivity, and overall satisfaction in the workplace by utilizing customized techniques and approaches that cater to their specific needs.

Effective time management is crucial for achieving success in the workplace. People diagnosed with ADHD frequently experience challenges in accurately perceiving time and may encounter difficulties in prioritizing tasks and meeting deadlines. One effective approach for individuals with ADHD is to implement strategies that promote organization and productivity. This can be achieved by creating daily to-do lists, breaking tasks into smaller, more manageable steps, and leveraging digital tools such as calendars and reminders. By establishing achievable objectives and scheduling dedicated time slots for each task, individuals can effectively avoid procrastination and enhance their overall productivity.

Efficient organization plays a crucial role in achieving success in the workplace. People with ADHD often face challenges in maintaining order and managing clutter, which can hinder their ability to concentrate and accomplish tasks effectively. Organizational systems, such as file folders, color-coding, and labeling, can be implemented to assist individuals with ADHD in effectively managing documents, materials, and deadlines. Establishing an organized and uncluttered workspace can minimize disruptions and improve focus.

Strong communication skills are crucial for achieving success in any professional environment. People with ADHD may face difficulties such as impulsivity, distractibility, or challenges in expressing themselves clearly. Engaging effectively in conversations and meetings can be facilitated by practicing active listening, asking clarifying questions, and summarizing key points. These strategies can be particularly helpful for individuals with ADHD. In addition, it is important to be aware of nonverbal cues such as eye contact, body language, and tone of voice. These factors can greatly improve communication and help build positive relationships with colleagues and supervisors.

Many individuals with ADHD struggle to maintain focus and concentration in the workplace. Utilizing techniques like the Pomodoro Technique can be beneficial for individuals with

ADHD as it allows for focused work intervals followed by short breaks, helping to sustain attention and prevent burnout. To enhance focus and productivity, it is recommended to utilize noise-canceling headphones, implement measures to block distracting websites or apps, and establish a dedicated workspace to minimize distractions.

Having a strong sense of self-awareness and the ability to advocate for oneself are essential skills for achieving success in the workplace, especially for individuals with ADHD. Having a clear understanding of one's strengths, weaknesses, and preferred work styles can be instrumental in helping individuals with ADHD effectively leverage their unique abilities and successfully navigate challenges. Advocating for reasonable accommodations, such as flexible work hours, ergonomic workstations, or assistive technologies, can provide individuals with ADHD with the necessary support to optimize their performance.

Developing strong professional relationships with colleagues and supervisors is crucial for achieving success in the workplace. Enhancing interpersonal skills can be beneficial for individuals with ADHD. One way to achieve this is by practicing empathy, active listening, and conflict resolution. Receiving feedback from supervisors and colleagues, providing assistance to others, and actively participating in team-building activities can greatly assist individuals with ADHD in establishing themselves as valuable contributors to the workplace community.

Ongoing learning and professional development are crucial for achieving success in the workplace, irrespective of an individual's ADHD status. Keeping up with current industry trends, acquiring new skills, and actively seeking opportunities for career advancement can greatly contribute to job satisfaction and facilitate professional growth. Individuals diagnosed with ADHD may find it advantageous to explore various resources, including workshops, seminars, online courses, and mentorship programs, to enhance their understanding and proficiency in managing their condition.

It is crucial to maintain a healthy work-life balance in order to promote overall well-being and achieve success in the workplace. People diagnosed with ADHD may have a tendency to take on too many responsibilities or become excessively focused on work-related tasks, which can negatively impact their personal lives. To effectively manage ADHD and prevent burnout, it is important for individuals to establish clear boundaries between work and leisure time. This can be achieved by implementing a structured schedule that includes regular breaks. Additionally, prioritizing self-care activities such as exercise, engaging in hobbies, and socializing can greatly contribute to recharging and maintaining overall well-being.

Having the ability to adapt and bounce back from challenges is crucial for achieving success in a professional setting.

People with ADHD may experience setbacks, challenges, or unexpected changes in their work environment. Individuals with ADHD can overcome obstacles and thrive in dynamic work environments by being adaptable, resourceful, and willing to learn from mistakes.

In order to achieve success in the workplace, individuals with ADHD must possess a set of essential skills. These include effective time management, organization, communication, focus, self-awareness, and interpersonal skills. Individuals with ADHD can maximize their potential and achieve success in their careers by implementing various techniques. These include creating to-do lists, organizing workspaces, practicing active listening, utilizing focus strategies, advocating for accommodations, building positive relationships, pursuing professional development, maintaining work-life balance, and cultivating flexibility and resilience. Individuals with ADHD have the potential to excel in the workplace and make valuable contributions to their organizations when they are supported with dedication and perseverance.

Learning Strategies for ADHD Students

Achieving academic success for students with ADHD is heavily dependent on implementing effective learning strategies that are specifically designed to address their individual needs and challenges. ADHD has a significant impact on multiple areas of learning, such as attention, organization, time management, and impulse control. Nevertheless, by implementing effective strategies, students diagnosed with ADHD can surmount these challenges and attain academic triumph.

Establishing routines and structure is a fundamental learning strategy for students with ADHD. Establishing consistent routines can assist students in fostering a sense of stability and predictability, ultimately reducing feelings of overwhelm and anxiety. Creating a structured study schedule, arranging study materials systematically, and dividing tasks into more manageable segments can assist students with ADHD in maintaining focus and staying on track.

Incorporating visual aids and organizers can be a beneficial approach for students who have ADHD. Utilizing visual learning tools, such as charts, diagrams, and graphic organizers, can greatly enhance students' ability to grasp intricate concepts and improve their retention of information. Utilizing color-coding techniques, employing sticky notes or index cards for reminders, and developing visual schedules can significantly improve organization and time management abilities.

Utilizing active learning techniques that engage multiple senses can prove highly advantageous for students diagnosed with ADHD. Engaging students in the learning process is facilitated through hands-on activities, group discussions, and interactive learning exercises. These methods encourage active participation and help maintain student engagement. Implementing movement breaks, kinesthetic learning activities, and integrating music or rhythm into study sessions can be beneficial for students with ADHD in maintaining focus and attention.

It is crucial to implement strategies that enhance attention and concentration in order to achieve academic success. It is recommended that students with ADHD consider dividing their study sessions into shorter intervals, allowing for frequent breaks to recharge and refocus. Using tools like timers, alarms, or apps that offer auditory cues can assist students in effectively managing their time and staying focused during study sessions.

Developing effective study habits and strategies is crucial for the success of students with ADHD. By instructing students on the importance of prioritizing tasks, setting goals, and developing study plans, they can gain the necessary skills to assume responsibility for their own learning and academic advancement. To enhance retention and comprehension, it is recommended that students review material regularly, practice active recall techniques, and utilize mnemonic devices.

Creating a conducive learning environment is crucial for students with ADHD to excel academically. Teachers have the ability to implement various classroom accommodations to meet the needs of students with ADHD. These accommodations may include preferential seating, designated quiet workspaces, or additional time for completing assignments or tests. Providing precise instructions, offering regular feedback, and giving praise and encouragement can also contribute to creating a supportive and motivating environment for students with ADHD.

Providing students with strategies to effectively manage impulsivity and regulate emotions can significantly enhance their academic performance. Various techniques, including deep breathing exercises, mindfulness practices, and cognitive-behavioral strategies, can assist students with ADHD in effectively managing stress, anxiety, and frustration. Teaching students effective strategies to identify and address negative thought patterns, as well as developing coping mechanisms to navigate setbacks, can foster resilience and perseverance.

It is crucial to engage in collaboration with parents, caregivers, and support professionals in order to effectively support students with ADHD in their academic pursuits. Establishing regular communication channels between educators and parents is crucial for maintaining consistency in expectations and support strategies across home and school environments. Consulting with professionals in the field of psychology, counseling, or other relevant specialties can offer valuable perspectives and resources to effectively address the unique requirements of students with ADHD.

It is essential to prioritize the development of a growth mindset and the cultivation of a positive attitude towards learning for students with ADHD. Highlighting the importance of effort, progress, and resilience rather than fixating on perfection can foster a sense of self-efficacy and motivation in students, encouraging them to persevere when confronted with difficulties. Recognizing achievements, acknowledging advancements, and offering platforms for students to demonstrate their abilities can enhance their self-assurance and academic performance.

To promote academic success, it is crucial to develop learning strategies that take into account the unique strengths, challenges, and needs of students with ADHD. Students with ADHD can maximize their potential and thrive academically by implementing various strategies. These include establishing routines and structure, using visual aids and organizers, engaging in active learning techniques, improving attention and concentration, developing effective study habits, creating a supportive learning environment, teaching self-regulation skills, collaborating with stakeholders, fostering a growth mindset, and cultivating a positive attitude toward learning. Students with ADHD have the potential to overcome obstacles and achieve their academic goals when provided with the necessary support, guidance, and encouragement.

CHAPTER 6

REFLECTIVE AND INTERACTIVE EXERCISES

Self-Evaluation Tasks

Self-evaluation tasks are important elements of exercises that encourage personal growth, self-awareness, and development. These tasks require individuals to carefully analyze their thoughts, emotions, actions, strengths, weaknesses, and experiences in different areas of their lives. Through the process of self-evaluation, individuals can acquire valuable insights into their own abilities, pinpoint areas that require improvement, and make well-informed decisions regarding their objectives and actions.

The main goal of self-evaluation tasks is to promote self-awareness. Self-awareness entails developing a comprehensive comprehension of one's own thoughts, emotions, motivations, and behaviors. Self-evaluation tasks allow individuals to analyze their beliefs, values, and attitudes and understand how these factors impact their actions and interactions with others. By understanding the inner workings of their own processes, individuals can make more informed decisions and ensure that their actions are in line with their objectives and principles.

Self-evaluation tasks are valuable for promoting personal growth and development. Through careful analysis of previous experiences, both positive and negative, individuals can gain valuable insights into patterns, trends, and opportunities for growth and development. These insights can be utilized to guide the development of strategies, goals, and action plans that are focused on improving skills, overcoming obstacles, and achieving desired outcomes. Engaging in regular self-evaluation can cultivate a mindset of ongoing learning and growth, motivating individuals to reach their maximum potential.

Self-evaluation tasks serve an important purpose in promoting accountability and responsibility. By assuming responsibility for their thoughts, emotions, and behaviors, individuals can acknowledge the influence they exert on themselves and those around them. Self-evaluation tasks prompt individuals to carefully consider the impact of their decisions, evaluate their role in different scenarios, and proactively address any unfavorable results. This sense of accountability promotes a feeling of agency and empowerment, enabling individuals to assume control of their lives and effectuate beneficial transformations.

Self-evaluation tasks offer individuals the chance to evaluate their progress towards their goals and objectives. Setting clear, measurable goals and regularly evaluating progress allows individuals to track their achievements, celebrate successes, and identify areas that require further effort or adjustment. Self-evaluation tasks allow individuals to assess their performance, make any necessary adjustments, and maintain motivation and focus on their goals.

In addition, self-evaluation tasks promote the development of a growth mindset, which involves believing in one's ability to learn, grow, and adapt. By approaching failures and setbacks as valuable learning experiences, individuals can navigate challenges with resilience and determination. Self-evaluation tasks encourage individuals to carefully consider their experiences, extract valuable lessons, and apply these insights to future endeavors. This change in mindset promotes a favorable outlook on personal growth and motivates individuals to view challenges as chances for advancement.

Self-evaluation tasks can be designed in different ways, depending on the specific goals and objectives of the exercise. Various methods are commonly employed in self-evaluation tasks, including written reflections, journaling, self-assessment questionnaires, goal-setting exercises, and seeking feedback from others. These tasks can be performed either individually or in group settings, depending on the desired outcomes and context. Irrespective of the format, it is crucial to encourage individuals to participate in sincere, introspective contemplation and offer necessary guidance and support.

Self-evaluation tasks have significant benefits in fostering self-awareness, personal growth, accountability, and goal achievement. Through the utilization of reflective and interactive exercises, individuals have the opportunity to acquire valuable insights into themselves, evaluate their progress towards their goals, and foster a growth mindset. Engaging in regular self-evaluation can cultivate a sense of agency and empowerment, allowing individuals to assume control over their lives and enact beneficial transformations. Self-evaluation tasks play a crucial role in a comprehensive approach to personal development and well-being.

Setting Objectives and Monitoring Results

Establishing goals and tracking outcomes are essential elements of reflective and interactive activities designed to foster personal and professional growth. The processes entail establishing precise and quantifiable goals or objectives, delineating strategies to accomplish them, and consistently assessing progress and results. Through the practice of structured goal-setting and regular monitoring, individuals can gain clarity on their priorities, effectively track their performance, and make well-informed decisions regarding their actions and behaviors.

To begin the process of setting objectives, it is important to first identify clear and specific goals that are in line with one's values, aspirations, and desired outcomes. The goals should be easily understood, attainable, and quantifiable, enabling individuals to monitor their progress and assess their achievements. It is crucial to clearly express objectives related to personal growth, career advancement, academic achievement, or other areas of life in order to provide direction and focus.

After establishing objectives, the subsequent step involves developing a plan or strategy to accomplish them. One approach is to break down larger goals into smaller, more manageable tasks. It is also important to identify resources and support systems that can assist in achieving these goals. Additionally, setting deadlines or milestones can help track progress along the way. By providing a clear and structured plan, individuals can establish a roadmap to effectively achieve their goals and successfully navigate any challenges that may arise.

It is crucial to regularly monitor results to ensure individuals stay on track towards their goals and make any necessary adjustments. One approach to this task is to monitor key performance indicators, gather data on progress and outcomes, and then analyze the actual results against predetermined benchmarks or targets. Through a methodical assessment of performance and outcomes, individuals can pinpoint areas for improvement, leverage successes, and tackle any challenges or setbacks that may arise.

An effective approach to setting objectives and monitoring results is the SMART criteria. This method provides a clear and structured framework for goal-setting. By ensuring that objectives are specific, measurable, achievable, relevant, and time-bound, organizations can increase their chances of success and track progress objectively. Implementing the SMART criteria requires expertise in goal-setting and a formal approach to ensure clarity and precision in defining objectives. The acronym SMART represents the following criteria: specific, measurable, achievable, relevant, and time-bound. By applying these criteria, one can ensure that goals are clearly defined, attainable, and actionable, thereby enhancing the chances of achieving success. Having clear and specific goals is essential for providing clarity and focus. It is important to set goals that are measurable so that progress can be tracked effectively. Additionally, setting achievable goals helps establish realistic expectations. It is also crucial to ensure that goals are relevant and aligned with one's priorities. Lastly, setting time-bound goals helps establish deadlines for completion.

Accountability is a crucial aspect of setting objectives and monitoring results. Through the act of sharing goals with others, seeking feedback, and actively soliciting support, individuals can effectively hold themselves accountable for their actions and outcomes. Having accountability partners, mentors, or coaches can be highly beneficial for individuals as they offer valuable guidance and encouragement and help in maintaining a strong sense of commitment towards their objectives.

Reflection plays a crucial role in the process of establishing objectives and tracking outcomes. Engaging in regular self-reflection enables individuals to gain valuable insights into their progress, achievements, and challenges. This practice helps identify strengths, weaknesses, and areas for improvement. Engaging in reflective exercises, such as journaling, self-assessment, or seeking feedback, can offer valuable opportunities for self-reflection and personal development. These activities foster self-awareness and facilitate meaningful growth.

Seeking feedback from others is a valuable practice that can provide different perspectives and insights, in addition to self-reflection. Receiving feedback from peers, mentors, supervisors, or colleagues can provide valuable insights into an individual's performance and effectiveness. Providing constructive feedback enables individuals to gain insights into their blind spots, acknowledge areas that require improvement, and enhance their strategies for achieving objectives.

When setting objectives and monitoring results, it is crucial to possess qualities such as flexibility and adaptability. Unforeseen obstacles, shifts in circumstances, or fresh insights may necessitate individuals to adapt their goals or strategies accordingly. Embracing feedback, learning from experiences, and being open to change enable individuals to effectively navigate uncertainties and overcome obstacles with resilience and agility.

Recognizing achievements and reaching significant milestones is crucial for sustaining motivation and progress. Acknowledging progress, achievements, and accomplishments serves as a source of positive reinforcement and strengthens a sense of fulfillment. Recognizing achievements motivates individuals to maintain their dedication and determination towards their goals, even when confronted with obstacles or setbacks.

Establishing goals and tracking outcomes are crucial steps in fostering personal and professional growth. Through the establishment of precise and quantifiable objectives, the development of strategies to attain them, and the consistent assessment of progress and results, individuals can enhance their understanding of priorities, monitor their performance, and make well-informed choices regarding their actions and conduct. By employing introspection, taking responsibility, adapting to change, and acknowledging successes, individuals can confidently and resiliently navigate the path of personal development and accomplishment.

CHAPTER 7

IN SUMMARY, YOUR JOURNEY TO BECOME AN ADHD SUPERPOWER

Long-Term Plans for Consistent Achievement

Developing and implementing long-term strategies is crucial in the process of harnessing the potential of ADHD and turning it into a strength. In addition to addressing the daily management of ADHD symptoms and implementing immediate strategies, it is essential to establish a plan for long-term success. These plans include a variety of strategies, habits, and approaches that aim to promote ongoing growth, progress, and fulfillment in different areas of life.

Goal setting is a crucial aspect of developing long-term plans for consistent achievement. Setting precise and significant goals offers guidance and purpose, directing individuals with

ADHD towards their desired results. These goals can encompass various areas, such as academics, professional growth, personal development, relationships, and health. Setting goals that are specific, measurable, achievable, relevant, and time-bound (SMART) allows individuals to establish a clear framework for success and effectively monitor their progress over time.

Furthermore, when aiming for consistent achievement, it is crucial to not only establish goals but also cultivate strategies and habits that foster sustained progress. Some areas to focus on may involve developing strong organizational skills, refining time management techniques, strengthening self-regulation and impulse control, and sharpening executive functioning abilities. Through the adoption of effective coping mechanisms and productivity techniques, individuals with ADHD can enhance their performance and overcome challenges more easily.

Maintaining consistency is crucial for individuals with ADHD to achieve long-term success. Creating and implementing routines, habits, and systems that encourage consistency can be instrumental in sustaining progress and minimizing obstacles. One possible approach is to create daily schedules, prioritize tasks, break larger goals into smaller, manageable steps, and establish regular review and reflection practices. Consistency and dedication to personal development are crucial for attaining long-term outcomes.

Taking care of oneself and maintaining a sense of well-being are crucial aspects of any long-term plan aimed at achieving consistent success. It is crucial to prioritize stress management, physical health, and mental wellness in order to sustain energy, focus, and motivation in the long run. Integrating activities like exercise, mindfulness, relaxation techniques, and sufficient sleep into daily routines can assist individuals with ADHD in rejuvenating and replenishing their resources, thereby improving resilience and overall well-being.

Establishing a support network is a crucial component of developing long-term strategies for sustained success. Having a strong network of supportive individuals, including friends, family members, mentors, or support groups, can offer valuable encouragement, guidance, and accountability. Obtaining professional support, such as therapy or coaching, can provide valuable insights and strategies for effectively managing ADHD symptoms and navigating challenges.

Ongoing learning and skill development are crucial for achieving sustained growth and success. Investing in education, training, and personal development initiatives allows individuals with ADHD to broaden their knowledge, gain new skills, and adjust to evolving circumstances. Continuing education, whether obtained through formal schooling, professional certifications, online courses, or self-directed learning, helps individuals build confidence, improve competence, and enhance adaptability.

Adaptability and resilience are essential qualities for effectively managing the challenges that come with ADHD. It is crucial to acknowledge setbacks, derive lessons from failures, and embrace change in order to effectively overcome obstacles and emerge even stronger. Developing a growth mindset promotes resilience and encourages individuals to see challenges as chances for growth and development. It is a belief in one's ability to learn and improve.

It is crucial to regularly engage in self-reflection and make necessary adjustments in order to maintain consistent progress towards long-term goals. It is important for individuals to regularly assess their progress, reevaluate their goals, and make necessary adjustments to their strategies based on feedback and experiences. This allows them to stay on track and ensure their continued success. Reflective practices, such as journaling, meditation, or coaching sessions, offer valuable opportunities for self-reflection and personal growth.

Recognizing and acknowledging milestones and successes is crucial for sustaining motivation and boosting morale. Acknowledging accomplishments, regardless of their magnitude, reinforces forward movement and fosters ongoing dedication and determination. There are various ways to celebrate, ranging from individual achievements and recognitions to collective moments with friends and family, which can promote a feeling of fulfillment and contentment.

To achieve consistent long-term success, it is crucial to establish meaningful goals, implement effective strategies and habits, prioritize self-care and well-being, foster a strong support network, invest in continuous learning and development, cultivate adaptability and resilience, engage in regular self-reflection and course correction, and celebrate milestones and successes. By adopting these principles and practices, individuals with ADHD can begin a path of ongoing development, advancement, and satisfaction, ultimately utilizing their distinctive strengths to become formidable assets in their personal lives.

Motivation and Hope for the Future

Having a strong sense of motivation and maintaining hope for the future are essential factors in effectively harnessing ADHD as a superpower. When dealing with ADHD, it is crucial to maintain motivation and cultivate a sense of hope. These factors are essential for staying resilient, focused, and optimistic about the possibilities that lie ahead. When summarizing the journey toward becoming an ADHD superpower, it is crucial to comprehend the dynamics of motivation and hope. This understanding is essential for maintaining progress and achieving one's maximum potential.

Motivation is a crucial factor that influences actions and behaviors, providing individuals with the necessary drive to pursue their goals and aspirations. Individuals with ADHD often face difficulties in maintaining motivation due to the fluctuating nature of attention, focus, and energy levels. By gaining a comprehensive understanding of the various factors that impact motivation and implementing effective strategies to bolster it, individuals can successfully navigate obstacles and maintain unwavering commitment to their personal journey of self-improvement and growth.

An essential aspect of sustaining motivation involves establishing precise and significant objectives that align with an individual's core values and aspirations. When goals are in harmony with personal interests and desires, individuals are more inclined to be motivated to pursue them. In addition, dividing larger goals into smaller, more manageable tasks can help reduce feelings of overwhelm and enhance the likelihood of success. This approach can boost motivation and maintain a steady momentum towards accomplishing the overall objective.

Another crucial element of motivation involves cultivating a sense of purpose and significance in one's endeavors. When individuals diagnosed with ADHD have a clear understanding of the importance of their goals and how they contribute to their overall well-being and fulfillment, they are more likely to maintain their motivation, even when faced with challenges. Developing a sense of purpose entails establishing a connection between goals and personal values, passions, and aspirations, emphasizing their significance and applicability.

In addition, it is worth noting that intrinsic motivation, which originates from within oneself, can have a significant impact on individuals with ADHD. When individuals derive pleasure, contentment, and a sense of accomplishment from their endeavors, they are more inclined to maintain their motivation in the long run. Promoting intrinsic motivation requires nurturing autonomy, competence, and relatedness, which are three psychological needs identified by self-determination theory. Additionally, it involves establishing environments that facilitate curiosity, creativity, and exploration.

Additional factors that can contribute to maintaining motivation for individuals with ADHD include external sources such as rewards, recognition, and social support. Receiving positive reinforcement, encouragement, and support from individuals such as friends, family members, peers, and mentors can be highly beneficial in navigating through difficult periods. In addition, implementing rewards or incentives for reaching milestones or finishing tasks can assist in sustaining motivation and cultivating a feeling of achievement.

The concept of hope for the future is deeply connected to motivation, acting as a guiding light of positivity and potential amidst the obstacles faced by individuals living with ADHD. Hope encompasses the belief in one's capacity to overcome challenges, accomplish objectives, and cultivate a satisfying existence, even in the face of setbacks and adversity. Nurturing hope requires fostering a positive perspective, resilience, and a mindset focused on growth. This entails perceiving challenges as chances for personal development and learning.

To cultivate optimism for the future, it is important to establish attainable goals and prioritize advancement rather than striving for flawlessness. Acknowledging and commemorating small achievements, regardless of their significance, can foster self-assurance and strengthen a positive outlook. In addition, viewing setbacks as temporary challenges rather than impossible obstacles can assist individuals in maintaining a positive outlook and strong determination when confronted with difficulties.

An essential element in fostering hope is establishing a support network comprised of individuals who have faith in one's abilities and provide encouragement, guidance, and validation. Being in the company of positive influences and role models who have successfully overcome similar challenges can be a source of inspiration and reassurance. In addition, it can be beneficial to seek professional support, such as therapy or coaching, to gain access to valuable tools and strategies for effectively managing the symptoms of ADHD and successfully navigating the challenges of life.

Visualizing success and envisioning a more promising future can also enhance hope and motivation for individuals with ADHD. Participating in practices like visualization, goal setting, and positive affirmations can assist individuals in clarifying their aspirations, strengthening their dedication to their goals, and fostering a sense of hope and optimism. By considering the potential outcomes that await, individuals can maintain their motivation and concentration on their path to harnessing the strengths associated with ADHD.

In summary, the presence of motivation and a positive outlook on the future are crucial elements in the process of embracing ADHD as a unique strength. By gaining a comprehensive understanding of the various factors that impact motivation, individuals with ADHD can effectively navigate their challenges and achieve their goals. This can be achieved by setting meaningful objectives, fostering intrinsic motivation, seeking external support, and cultivating a sense of hope. By implementing these strategies, individuals with ADHD can maintain their momentum and unlock their full potential. By maintaining a strong sense of determination, resilience, and a positive outlook, individuals can effectively navigate the challenges of living with ADHD and ultimately cultivate a fulfilling and meaningful life.

www.ingramcontent.com/pod-product-compliance
Lightning Source LLC
Chambersburg PA
CBHW022138150726
47992CB00002B/653